The Peace of Courage

MEMOIRS OF A RECOVERING COWARD

ANNICE SILIMON

The Peace of Courage: Memoirs of a recovering coward

Publisher: Carlion Publishers

Editing: Cynthia Tucker
Proofreading and Typesetting: Sally Hanan at Inksnatcher.com
Cover Design: Sherilyn at CamdenLaneCreative.com

Ordering Information: Quantity sales. Special discounts are available on quantity purchases by corporations, associations, and others. For details, contact the author at the email address above.

The Peace of Courage: Memoirs of a recovering coward/Annice Silimon
ISBN 978-1-7329652-3-2

This book is dedicated to you, the reader. May you forever know the peace of courage.

Contents

Foreword

Annice, I recommended that you write this book. You fought it, but I knew it was time. I am so grateful to be a part of your journey of rediscovery and triumph. I am proud of where the Lord has taken you and what he has done in your life in these three short years. I am amazed at your tenacity and strength. You have overcome something that many never do. This book embodies a strength some will never understand. Divorce is a hard topic to discuss, but abuse is a silent killer. The grief that accompanies these things is immeasurable. Your opening your mouth to speak is a game changer.

Reader, this book is a game changer. Readers delve deep into the secrets and truths of this author. It is sure to change your life and perspective of life's problems, for the better. Annice challenges literary rules and bears hear soul. This is not a traditional self-help book; it is an opportunity to see the world from a once broken woman. She lets us into the dark and deep places.

She faces fear, and causes the reader to do so as well. Welcome to courage.

Dr. Alexis Maston-McClinton

CEO of Carlion Publishing

Preface

THAT URGE. THE MOMENT when you are hit with inspiration to do something out of the ordinary. For a split second, you catch a glimpse of the behemoth of a human…a superhuman, invincible, indivisible, and invisible.

You hesitate. I hesitate. The urge passes. We shrink. We whisper words that curse our souls because once again, we have dropped the ball of greatness. If I could, if I should, if I did.

My life as I know it would not exist. I would run with the kings and queens upon the high and lofty places, yet here we sit among the lowly, the paupers, the lilies who die while yet in bloom.

It is the dialogue of efficacy in doubt. We all have internalized the moment of hate at some point in time. Digested a self-based truth of low esteem, no respect for the coward that keeps showing up. We flounce before people as though if and when the opportunity for bravery presents itself, we are well able to lead the charge. However, we flounder through the seats of our souls, listening to the voice of remembering and recounting the last time.

Courage—

The power to face what scares, pains, endangers, or grieves you.

Power—

The ability, the strength, the grit; the audacity.

Courage is the audacity to be daring. Courage has nothing to do with acumen, skill, talent, or discipline. Courage is the wild, untamed donkey waiting for the chance to break free and dance upon the high places. Courage will overtake skill and ability. Courage is haughty at times because she is unstoppable. Courage is headstrong, refuses to count the cost—always ready for the moment to take center stage and be free.

Courage has nothing to do with worthiness or readiness. Courage is the ever-present opportunity not waiting for an opportunity. Courage lives in your heart.

I am Annice.

I know what it is like to be a coward on the outside and a lion on the inside.

Scared of what people may think. Scared to show the world the truth.

Scared to live my truth. Scared to write this story. That's why it has taken me four years to do so.

I know what it's like to look out into the world and wish that you could bring more.

Yet, sit still.

Be quiet.

Do nothing

Not because you can't but because you are caged.

I am Annice, and I'm a recovering coward.

I'm still on the road. I'm getting there—free.

I'm still on the road of being courageous.

I don't know what started it. The hesitation, cowering in the corner, keeping quiet when you want to speak up. I don't remember the first time I started playing the role—being small. I guess in my head, I lived in another dimension where I was a giant, where I was a force—and then I would look at myself in the mirror of life and see myself. I was a grasshopper, an ant, a speck.

Invisible.

I don't know when it started, but I decided that it was ending. I decided to walk this road—a road of transparency—because I feel like I can help some people who also deal with being courageous and fearless.

Honestly, I don't know if anybody ever knows what they fear.

I don't know if anybody can give an honest answer to why we are genuinely hesitant to bring our voices to the market, or this generation. Why do we hesitate to pour our lives out into the world?

I don't know.

What I do know is this: you serve no one by being small.

You serve no one when you hesitate at the moments of opportunity for courage.

Perhaps if I go first and start the conversation about what I'm living, it may shed light on what you're living, and together we could forge a community. We could be a community of people who are recovering and transforming.

We could become a tribe of the courageous.

Herein is a script, a scroll of my soul, a letter of love to your dark places.

I am Annice. I am finding the peace in being courageous.

Annice Silimon

The Beginning Is the End

— 1 —

Courage is the forgotten seat of the soul.

THUD. CREAK. CRUNCH. The sound of my phone being thrown down a flight of stairs and hitting a wall, striking the recently swept hardwood floor face down.

Vicious curse words accompany these sounds. This particular episode is spurred by the desire of my ex-husband to speak to his kid. His kid who is now being treated more like a stepson by the voice that is screaming at the top of the stairs.

How in the world did I get here? Clearly, this cannot be heaven on earth. I sit here, face in my hands, staring off into space oblivious to the cussing and cursing. I am immune, and I am numb. I am done.

Tears are rolling down my cheeks. Silently I sit and cry. I am not crying for my marriage. Instead, I am crying out for the release of divorce. I have given up hope. I have been cussed at, stolen from, manipulated, lied to, and I am now ready to admit—there is no hope here.

I married the personality of my mother. I ran from the angry sounds of childhood only to crash into the same anger encapsulated and unleashed in a supposed life partner.

Life partner?

Please. I would rather be dead than deal with this, at least that's what I told myself.

This story of finding courage starts at the end of a horrible marriage—the D-Word, Divorce.

We had been married for a short time and didn't have a dating period. After the separation, as I was walking toward the finality of divorce, I didn't know it was the beginning of the end of life as I knew it. Anybody who has divorced knows that there is the mourning of the death; there is the mourning of expectation. Nobody wants to find themselves facing divorce and being left with nothing. When you're walking toward separation, you're optimistic about getting a fresh start. After it's over, you are happy to be out of there—glad to be gone.

December 19, 2015, was my moving day.

My current home is across the bridge from where I was living at the time. The bottom began to fall out on New Year's Eve, a few weeks after my official moving day.

It's one thing when you think you've hit rock bottom, but it's another thing when you see that rock bottom also has a bottom, and it's getting ready to fall out. In our relationship, there were some narcissistic tendencies, and I didn't feel the blows of something like that until I was gone. Where I was once optimistic about getting out and starting over, I started seeing the blows. It's almost like an action movie where they're continuously fighting. They get shot, they get stabbed, but they keep fighting. It's not until somebody comes up to them and says, "Oh my gosh! You're bleeding; are you okay?" That's how it was. You pull back the shirt and see all these other wounds you had not accounted for when making the transition.

Depression

The cycles of abuse. Sure, I'd read the pamphlets over the years, and watched the movies about women who were married to absolute jerks, but how did I get here? How in the world did an honor student with everything but a dissertation get into an abusive relationship? I must have forgotten that abuse victims aren't categorized by education or socioeconomics because abuse doesn't know identifiers. The thing that got me was that I am strong. I am amazing, and I somehow fell for the complete and utter bamboozlement of all bamboozlement. This man may have never loved me. Shoot, did I ever love me? I had to. My rationale for this goes back and forth, I am a sitting duck, waiting for an answer to come to me. Then it hits me; this man couldn't love the other women that he was with or me because, well because he wasn't really straight.

Let that sink in.

I was a mark. I was a beard. I was a cover and a front.

I was not his wife.

I was not his choice.

I take responsibility NOW. I do not blame him for being him. I own the fact I entered freely (even if I could not see what was purposefully being withheld) into a life with this behavior.

I am not a victim.

I am a woman who went through a series of events. Events which would be the key to unlock the brokenness hiding beneath the surface.

I admit I loved him. I loved my first husband. I was committed to the concept of marriage.

I

was

committed.

I own my part because I needed to sit and heal from the first marriage (which was a long relationship), but instead I jumped heart first into a situation that promised to be everything I never had in a relationship.

That is exactly what it was.

I had to come to terms that I, Annice, was in an abusive marriage—an abusive situation that seemed beautiful and perfect when we first met. I had to come to terms that I had wounds, and due to the mental, emotional, and financial injuries, the bottom to the bottom began to fall out. It was the beginning of the end, not of life as I knew it, but of Annice as I knew her. I didn't realize then that God was using a situation and people close to me to transition me into the person he needed me to be.

In January of the following year, I started slowly drifting into depression. I have experienced melancholy states before—we all have. But there's a difference between going through a season of sadness or brokenness and entering a full-blown depressed state. People often get the two confused. It's one thing to grieve properly for a while, but it is another thing when you spiral to a place that's not easy to get out of, and you have to deal with the aftermath connected to that depressive state.

Nobody knew I felt crazy. My dad passed away, my mom is alive, and I have one brother and one sister. Only my sister knew that I had gotten remarried and was going through a divorce

My dad was a fantastic person—an amazing dad, and so we weren't built for bad relationships. If you have an amazing dad, you're not built for bad relationships; you're made for good relationships. You're built to find people who look and sound like this rock in your life. He didn't introduce us to narcissistic behavior. He did not introduce us to or even exhibit abusive behavior. My mom was abusive; she was the narcissist, not my dad.

I didn't realize I had taken on the role of my father and had married someone like my mother. I loved my husband, but the person that I loved and married was not the person that I got to know. I was introduced to the real person about a month into the marriage, and once you've known somebody a certain way, it's hard to reframe that introduction.

The human brain wants to believe that what it first thought about a person is right. May Angelou said it best: "When somebody shows you who they are, believe them." It's hard to believe them when you've already been shown another personality, another character. You've experienced a different relationship. The man I fell in love with was not the man I married. I didn't know the signs of abuse even though I grew up in an abusive home. Since the abuse was female abuse, it was an outlier because everybody had great mothers in my life. It is not something you run into often, so I didn't even realize that behavior was present because I didn't know what I was witnessing.

Because I loved him, I excused his behavior when I was introduced to the real person. I excused it because I was a pastor; I excused it because there was so much stress; I excused it because he had experienced a loss in a previous marriage and was a single dad. I justified lousy behavior because I thought marriage was a place of healing and would naturally bring up things in us that were hidden or we hadn't addressed in a long time.

Four months later, I was completely confused. Anybody who has ever been in a narcissistic relationship knows that the highs are very high and the lows are very low, but you can track the circle. The circle is to keep you off your footing. I had never experienced something like this before, so I called my sister and brought her into the relationship. Within three months, she was tired of dealing with so much drama all the time.

Death

I remember vividly living in fear of having contracted HIV. I had always wondered if he was homosexual. Little moments seemed to stand still—I would watch in slow motion and dismiss them quickly. Surely, you're tripping, Annice, or was I?

One day I was getting ready for church. I looked in my mirror in the bathroom, and he was in front of his mirror. We could see each other's reflection in our mirrors. He stood. Stared. Almost to himself, he said, "I cannot believe I am married to someone who looks better than me." He always said narcissistic remarks like these, and I would ignore them.

I froze at the statement. What man wants to be more beautiful than his wife? The wife is the crown of the husband, right?

It wasn't long before he started putting me down and cursing me out. He hated me. He hated what I stood for, and he hated how I sounded. He hated my presence.

I loved him. I don't know why and maybe some love can't be explained, but I loved him. I loved his vision, and what he wanted to be as a pastor. I loved his children as if they were mine. I recall not having enough food to feed myself, but I would take what I had to feed the children. He was very distant, barely present; I felt alone.

I remember the moment, sitting alone, across the bridge in an overpriced condo, thinking what if he was sleeping with that man the whole time we were together?

Thoughts like these added to the deep wounds, I had a lot of questions. How did I not see this even though we went to marital counseling? I had fasted, and I was a preacher, a prophet, and a co-pastor, so how did I get like this? Depression is anger turned inward—that's all it is. I began to spiral into a place of thick, inward darkness. I then turned to drugs and alcohol, but I was a mother, I had businesses, I was finishing up a dissertation for a PhD, and I was not prepared for the hit that I took.

Now that I look back, I know that hindsight is twenty-twenty. I understand now that God allowed the situation to shatter my life. When something shatters, I usually get the big pieces, access the situation, and see what I can glue back together. But there are times when God is bringing you through something and doesn't want the pieces saved. Most of us, as we reach a certain age, fight with God when he wants to transform us when he says to leave a place. We fight with him because we're so comfortable where we are, so that's where I was.

If this hadn't happened to me, I would still be in the same place doing the same the thing with the same people. I felt I was living somebody else's life. During the time I was depressed, I wasn't bathing, I wasn't eating, and nobody knew what was going on. The people that I had done church with for fifty years or so walked away from me. Even though some people knew the story of how my husband operated, they still dropped me.

Nobody checked on me; there were no phone calls, so I became increasingly bitter. I wasn't even mad at the people. I was mad at my ex-husband and became angry with the Lord. That's where the real juice began to spill out and spill over, and that's where the real shattering, the real transformation, had to happen. There were some things I was carrying. I didn't just end up at this place, and I didn't just end up with these people—it was a cycle. It was like a cyclone that etches out a particular path, and we go along and don't realize we're doing it. I was angry with God. I felt I've tithed, and I've given, I've been there for your people, I've denied myself, I'm basically a martyr—how could you let me go through this? I should be exempt from the fiery furnace; I should be exempt because of all the good I've done for your name.

I went through this horrible, beautiful, terrible, amazing season. One day I said to the Lord, "Let me feel this so I don't change and so I can know I'm still alive. If I can feel the pain when I wake up the next day, there is hope that I will keep waking up and going to bed, and one day I'm going to wake up and find that I have passed through this tunnel." I think that was my first courageous yes when I sat before the Lord and said, "Just let me feel it; don't numb my emotions. Let me feel the anger and then let me deal with the anger. Let me feel bitterness and then let me deal with the bitterness." I prided myself on building prayer teams and teaching prayer and the secrets of prayer, but God smashed my prayer life because he was showing me all the things in me that were churchy, things that were not him. What I was going through had nothing to do with people, but it had everything to do with all of the doors that I left open for anger, bitterness, and craziness. I let them in the door and closed the door so that nobody could see them. I didn't want anyone to know that underneath the surface, behind the doors, I was medicating to give myself identity and personality.

NOTE TO SELF

That feeling you get when you want to run and hide in the plain sight.

That's how I feel today.

I am tired.

My life has to be a joke; only I am not laughing.

I am tired.

I am scared.

I am invisible. I am invisible. I am invisible.

The Peace of Courage

Wait.

Emotions are like unruly children. They need to be put in their place and trained.

My emotions are driving my fears, and my fears are driving my emotions.

A cyclone of a cycle...and I am drunk from the ride.

The moment when you are hit with inspiration to do something out of the ordinary. For a split second, you catch a glimpse of the behemoth of human…a superhuman, invincible, indivisible, and invisible.

What if right now I decided to rise up…scared?

What if in this very moment I fought back?

What if this one moment I pushed through?

Could I? Should I? Can I? Will I?

I can. I should. I will.

Even if I fail…the outcome is I came out.

Courage—the power to face what scares, pains, endangers, or grieves you.

Power—the ability, the strength, the grit—the audacity.

The Hebrew word *leb* means "soul" or "heart of man, conscience, seat of appetite, seat of emotions and passions, seat of courage."

The Beginning Is the End

We have been in error for eras. I thought courage was a thing I could possess, a behavior I could model, a sound emerging from beyond my realm of success.

You concluded courage was akin to risk—some adverse while others addicted.

We relied upon what we produced outwardly while all along, courage was coded into our DNA.

Courage is not just in you—courage is you.

Once we come to know, we can never return.

It was never that you were not enough. It was never that you were not talented enough. It was just that you and I were scared of the immense, vastly emerging and urgent request of an ancient well of great potential. The glimpses scared us—we were not used to seeing our truest selves with such clarity. We settled for the lie because it was easier, somewhat comforting. However, now we have been expelled from this nomadic nature of nugatory, and we have been invited to our true nature.

Courage.

- Annice, Circa 2014.

The Roots of the Foundation

— 2 —

Courage is not bravery alone...it is having to face the fear alone.

THIS WAS THE BEGINNING OF THE END of me, but the beginning of me started like everybody else, with foundations. I grew up in New Mexico where there were no deliverance ministers. No great people were traveling to New Mexico to teach deep mysteries in the eighties, at least if there were, I didn't know about them. My dad was a pastor, so we were in church all the time. My second-grade teacher was also part of our church. I got saved early on. In the church, we always heard, "You got to get to the root." A plant or tree has multiple roots, which is what makes the system. So this crashing, this clashing, this claiming, this breaking I experienced because of the divorce came from the fear I felt when I was a little girl.

Like most kids, I was gifted, but nobody saw it. That generation hadn't been introduced to the charismatic movement, which included dreams, visions, and prophecy. Prophecy in the seventies was sometimes even brought up as an enigma. In the eighties, it emerged as something more mainstream. I would dream vividly and walk around singing the songs of the Lord for hours, often making up words. Even though I was having these vivid dreams of the Lord, I wasn't an active dreamer. Dreams are just another dimension of living. Those gifts were there, but nobody was putting their hands on it. I would dream, I would sing the songs of the Lord, but I was using them as a way of escape. My imagination as a kid became the doorway to an agreement with the spirit of escapism.

The Cause

My mom was the second oldest of eighteen children. In her day, a set of grandparents would take one child, often the oldest girl, and that left my mom. As the oldest in the house, she took on the brunt of the responsibility of raising her siblings. Of course, we know siblings don't respect other siblings the way they respect their parents. My mom learned tactics just to survive and stay alive as the one running the household. I believe by the time she got us, and she was exhausted. She had been raising kids her whole life, and then she married my father and his life was completely different. She never really got to enjoy life; she never got to explore who she was, her identity. Would she ever get out of Atlanta? What did she want to do with her life besides going to nursing school? Being a nurse is great, but she didn't do it long and didn't have the time to explore.

When she married my father in her early twenties, her mom stopped speaking to her for a while. So there was this significant fraction in our family, and though she comes from a big family, we don't know any of them. We never had grandparents, we never had cousins, and we never had aunties. When it came to us, my mom did what she knew worked—she beat us to the point of unconsciousness. A lot of her soul hurt, and soul issues played out in the house.

We lived in constant dread and terror, so these things were already starting to attach themselves to us as we were learning to speak. We were afraid to make a sound; we were afraid of simple things. For instance, one time I had the flu and went to school with a high fever. We never wanted to be home, so even if we were sick, we tried to hide it to get out of the house.

While at school, I passed out and they called my mom. I knew I was going to be in trouble. They called me to the office, and my mom was standing there waiting to check me out. When we were walking down the hallway, she turned and punched me in the face because she had to come to the school because I was sick.

There was always this air of dread and fear among the siblings. Our childhood was really weird. When she wasn't home, we were free, but the moment we heard the key in the door, things changed. That's the typical story of abuse—behind closed doors.

At one time, you could not have told me my dad was not God. I thought he had to be God in the flesh again. There were times when my mom was beating us, and my dad stood in front of us to take the beating. He wouldn't yell, he would say nothing; never cussed, never screamed, and he never lifted his hand. He would sit there and take it. We saw blood running down his face as she cursed him out.

Clearly, these issues that she never had the chance to deal with were coming out. Marriage is supposed to be a place of healing, but she was trapped.

As a child, I got lost in my dreams and the songs of the Lord. I spent an enormous amount of time in my room by myself, sitting on the floor with two Barbie dolls in my hand. To an onlooker, it would appear I was sitting in silence while, in reality, I was traversing the lands of wild fantasies in my head. I did this for hours. I was already in agreement with the spirit of escapism.

Around age seven or eight, I began to be tormented in my dreams. The place where God is going to use us is the place the enemy tries to latch on to and destroy quickly. I would be awake but be unable to get out of the dream. I would be struggling, and in my dream, I would hear my mom's voice, tormenting me, saying, "Get up, get up," but I couldn't. That was my recurring nightmare.

My dad used to have Bible study on Wednesdays at the house. When he prayed for people, demons would come out of them. He wasn't trying to cast them out, and since he had no formal training, the demons were left in the house. We saw things—things came up missing, shadows were cast, stuff was on the ceiling, and doors closed on their own. At that age, I became terrified of the dark. From the age of seven to twenty-seven, I prayed the same prayer every single night: "Lord, do not let me see an angel and don't let me see one demon." I understood that if I saw one, I had to see the others. While I would love to see an angel—at one point I thought I did—I didn't want the repercussions. I didn't want to see a demon.

I was twenty-one and walking with God, but I still slept with all the lights on. I had night-lights everywhere and woke up hearing things. I was terrified, and this even seeped into my experiences with the Lord, so even my dreams had stopped. My dreams didn't kick back up until I was coming out of that divorce and going through the season of depression.

I was part of a lineage of dreamers, a lineage of prophets. My dad would tell this story of when he was in basic training in the Air Force. He went through a season where every night he wrestled with Satan on his bunk, which was on the bottom. The man on the top bunk was a Christian but never heard him wrestling and never woke up. My dad woke up with scratches, ripped up, so that's how he gave his life to Jesus.

When I was going through that season of breaking to be put back together, I also woke up wrestling and fighting. I had all these experiences because the season I was coming out of was meant to finally be the tipping point to taking me out completely. I wasn't supposed to live through it, I wasn't supposed to come through it, and I'm not supposed to be here writing this story. It was supposed to be over.

The spirit of escapism was still present when I transitioned to middle school. I didn't use Barbie dolls anymore, of course; instead, I read an enormous amount of content. We transitioned back to Atlanta, and my dad was working for a book distributor, so he got all these books for free and brought home boxes of books every day. I did my homework and then read two or three books at night. It wasn't normal to be able to read 700+ pages in two days, but I did. The way I digested information was not normal, but I felt I could live in the pages of those books. It was a way for me to escape what was going on in our home.

My brother was out of there when he graduated from Clark Atlanta, and my sister moved out when she was sixteen, so I was the only one left. My mom was older, but I still got a lot of her anger as she aged. She didn't hit me as much, but she would say things like, "You're stupid, you're ugly, you're a 'B,' you're a whore, you're this, you're that." Our interactions were limited because my head was literally stuck in a book. That was the only way I could escape fear. All these stories were shaping my world, and fear was really was shaping my identity.

The Coven

When spirits come, and the child agrees with these spirits, a covenant is forged. The spirits watch from then on to make sure the child is on a certain trajectory, whether this child was at church or work. Witchcraft was a thing, especially if you were from the South. It runs in my mom's family. Of course, we didn't know any aunties because she had cut them entirely off. For example, when her mother passed away, my mom didn't go to her funeral.

In high school, I didn't drink or do drugs, but the spirit of escapism and fear was driving my life. I graduated from high school a year late because I didn't attend my classes enough. I skipped a lot of school, but I was a straight-A student. That says a lot about the school system. I would show up and take tests, and teachers pulled me to the side and told me how brilliant I was. But they wouldn't see me for two weeks after that. I rode the bus to school, and CCTV public transportation had a bus stop right by the school. I got off my bus and took the city bus to Marta, the train in the city of Atlanta. Every day, all day, I rode the train from the beginning of the line to the end of the line until it was time for me to get back to the school, hop on my bus, and go home. When it was time to graduate, my behavior caught up with me. I took all my classes, I did all the coursework according to the standards, but I didn't have the necessary class time. I had to go to an alternate school and be a teacher's aide for several months. I then walked with the class graduating at that time.

When I was in eleventh grade and almost eighteen, I had my daughter. That's when I finally moved out, so I've been on my own for that long. I also have a son. I didn't have the wisdom to be on my own; that spirit of fear was driving, and I was running. I was running, and I was crashing, and I would get up and dust myself off, thinking only that I needed to keep running. I would run from one situation to another, but I know God was there.

I was hanging with crazy people. One year I went to the club, and a man walked up to me and said, "Why are you here? You're not even supposed to be here. You need to leave." I had all of these encounters repeatedly, but all I was trying to do was escape. Most people would be caught up in drugs, but I was looking for pockets of life where I could hide and watch the scenery. I was looking at life like it was a book. I didn't have to participate; all I had to do was watch the pictures.

I was finally on my own in my apartment, but for years, I had no furniture. I started working at a fast-food restaurant. I had become a manager at age sixteen when I was still in high school and still at home. My little girl's father and I were always cool; we were just in a bad situation. We were too young to know what we were doing. One day he and a friend started shooting guns at the apartment while I was at work. Because this was an apartment complex, they evicted him.

I stayed in the apartment a few more weeks—until the people came and the lights got cut off, and I knew I finally had to go.

I put four outfits in my trunk, and one of them was all white. I decided I needed to go to school because I needed to do something. I went to school for one year, homeless. I would catch showers here and there. My daughter was now living with her father's parents. I tried to hang on as long as I could during that first year of college, and I just couldn't. I remember thinking, *This is one situation, but I'm not going to rebound from, there is not a clear way of escape.*

I was twenty, and my brother and sister had both finished college and gotten married. My brother is an engineer, and both my brother and sister look like they did the right thing. I felt like I was just a statistic, only a number, another teen who messed up, so I would have to make my life work the best I could.

The whole time, fear was driving me. I was courageous and did crazy things because the gift of faith was always there. Somehow, even though I wasn't acknowledging God yet, I would be able to get knocked down, pop up, and keep running, crashing into more crazy behavior.

I started dating a Latino, and his mom was a big-time drug dealer in the area—when the drugs came over from Mexico, they went to her house. I started selling drugs. Since I didn't do them, I figured it would be 100 percent profit. Everybody else selling drugs cut into their profit margin by consuming them. I had a lot of friends who smoked, and I was the odd one out. I still didn't drink and didn't smoke, so I figured this was the perfect market for me. I believed that by selling dope, I was making the best out of a dead situation.

I was twenty-one, and we had just crossed over the millennium. One day my brother called and said, “Hey, we have to go see Daddy.” My mom and dad had abruptly moved to Alabama, and nobody knew why. Any time we called to talk to my father, he put us on the phone with our mother. Since we didn’t like her, we just got off the phone. We didn’t know what was going on. We were just like, “What’s this Alabama stuff?” My sister was in Italy, and my brother and I were living in Atlanta at the time. My daughter was about three. I didn’t know my brother had been in contact with my mom the whole time. He had seen some things, but he did not take them seriously because my dad was so like God when we were kids, in that we never knew of him ever being sick.

My brother and I made the hour-long trip. When we arrived, he walked in, and my mom went into a frenzy. She said my father had passed out a few times that morning. My mom and brother were fussing and arguing. I put my daughter in a chair and walked back to the bedroom. I saw my dad lying in bed, looking like he weighed eighty pounds. He didn't look like my dad. I thought *I don't know who this cat is, but this is not my dad.*

He asked me four questions: where was I, was I okay, what was I going to do, and was my daughter Tori okay and safe. I answered the questions, and it seemed that was all he wanted. He then wanted me to get my brother. My brother came and picked him up and took him to the bathroom to shower him. They were going to take him to the doctor.

I walked out dazed and confused, thinking, *What in the world is this?* I hadn't laid eyes on them for two years after they moved, but my dad was really like my bestie. After my brother and sister left, my dad had poured his wisdom into me. We went shopping, and he taught me how to shop. My dad was like most people's moms. For two years when I called him, he gave the phone to my mom, so I didn't understand what was going on.

My brother came out of the bathroom a minute later, angry and screaming, "This is crazy;

I'm calling 911." And he and my mom started going at it again. I ran into the bathroom, and my dad was lying on the floor. He was naked, I could see all of his bones, and he had stopped breathing. I gave him mouth to mouth until the paramedics showed up.

When the paramedics came to take him out of the room, I knew he was dead. I kneeled at a chair and said, "God, you still have time to take my mother and leave my father. What are you doing? Take her; leave him." But the paramedics pronounced my dad dead.

We went through the funeral and then returned to regular life. The next two years were a complete spiral for me.

The Enemy wanted me dead. I was supposed to die here.

Demonic covens and watchers were prominent in my life. This was one of those situations where I should have been completely taken out—I was not supposed to recover from this overwhelming loss. After the death of my father, I started bartending, and then I moved into club management super quick—unnaturally quick.

All this demonic stuff was present. There amidst the darkness, I started drinking and doing ecstasy for about a year. Again, I was trying to escape the finality that, in my mind, I didn't have any parents, I didn't have any family. My brother and sister have no issues with each other, but because of what we went through as children, we're just not close. When we get together or talk on the phone, we're good, but it seemed we had just run as far as we could to forget the past life to live our present life.

Note to Self

Brave One

I realize you walked into today perhaps not feeling as strong as you'd like. Your hopes for 2015 were once like firecrackers and now seem to have become as wet matches in your hand. Your gaze at the calendar has nothing to do with anticipating vacation; instead, it is the dread of crossing into December and realizing again you are occupying the same productivity seat as last year.

Brave One

You dream in color, but you resist—making black and white your default setting. You strive to be grounded and reprimand flighty thinking. What you once decided would be your contribution to humanity is rarely ever spoken of—yet you secretly admire the bold and brazen people who refuse to settle…for anything. You watch their fire and compare.

Brave One

Let me be the first to say I admire your strength. You have graduated from the University of Adversity with Honors. Impressive, I applaud you. I offer you a standing ovation. What you have accomplished through the moments of tightness and leanness is amazing. You have had nonexistent support for long seasons…you came through dark seasons which appeared to never end. I stand in awe of how sturdy you stand, consistent in your stance to just continue.

Brave One

I encourage you to continue to stand. I encourage you to keep dreaming regardless of how black and white they show up. I encourage you to pat yourself on the back. Throw yourself a party. *You decided* to get up this morning, even in the midst of your fears, frustrations, and faults. You decided your life is worth the attempt to move forward no matter how slow the process…no matter how slow the progress. Stay in the process, for you are making progress.

Brave One

The Peace of Courage

I name your name with authenticity and sincerity. You have proven you belong where you decide to show up. I understand you feel like an imposter, a poser, and a fake. Well, so do I. So do we all. We search the environment for courage. We scan the environment for the bravery of those who keep showing up scared, weary, and underestimated. Our search yielded you—the truth. The beautiful, simple truth: The world longs to admire the courageous, those who are journeying to a better place. We long to watch you win. We long to use your blaze to catch sparks of courage. You are a hero, a hero of courage because you decided to show up…today.

Brave One

- Annice, Circa 2015.

Faking It Ain't Making It

– 3 –

Courage is revealed with certainty in the comfort of pain.

I WAS TWENTY-ONE, and I didn't know anything about life. I was failing because I didn't have any wisdom. I had no one to say, "Child, you need to stop doing what you're doing." Eight months into bartending and club management, I worked in the most popular clubs in Atlanta on Saturday night. I knew everybody and met many celebrities; it was great. I would look out into the crowd of thousands of people, and I would see both people and spirits. It was like the veil started lifting, and I was beginning to see it.

On the weekends, I spent twenty-four hours in a partying environment. I left the strip club at 8 a.m. to bartend at the Gentleman's Club. I left there at 5 p.m. and went around the corner to another club, where I would stay from 7 until close. I left there around 8 a.m. I would have alcohol all over my clothes, and, of course, those clothes were inappropriate for any setting other than the club. I smelled like alcohol and cigarette ashes. I can only imagine what I must have smelled like to others, but in this season, I had to go to church. Do not pass go, do not collect two hundred dollars, do not go home and take a bath, and do not change your clothes—just go to church. I would show up at the church after twenty-four hours of being in the midst of shenanigans, smells, and spirits. I showed up in those same clothes. Nobody would talk to me, nobody would touch me, but I would stand in the pew.

I knew what worship was because of where I came from. It was as if the Holy Spirit said, "Now look, I'm taking this car, and you're going to church."

I was pretty faithful. I went every Sunday and some Tuesdays too, if I wasn't working. For me, it was the most epic battle. In the pew, fear would start talking to me, saying,

"You know you're a witch, right?

You know they're going to find you out, right?

You know you don't belong here, right?

You know you're evil, right?

You know demonic activity and darkness is all around you, and that's why they don't talk to you; that's why they don't touch you."

I would stand there while nobody talked to me or touched me. I stayed there, and that's where I got licensed to be a "coward" but ultimately licensed to be courageous. It was a prophetic house, but nobody saw or addressed the warfare present in the pew.

I was still bartending after a year and still doing drugs. I still went to church, high on drugs half the time, but I was faithful and eventually joined the church. On the day I was supposed to take the right hand of fellowship, I was ready; I was excited. I said, "I'm going to bed early because tomorrow, I'm going to be a member for real." My boyfriend said, "Come on, let's just drink and get high on ecstasy," and so I did it. I was drinking and was rolling; I got high.

I walked past the mirror and looked into it, and I heard this voice say, "What are you doing? What are you doing?" I was pulled immediately out of my high; I was no longer drunk. I stood there saying, "I don't know." I had no idea what I was doing or why I wanted to do it. The desire for drugs and alcohol left me right there...standing in front of the mirror hearing from God.

Just like that, the Father pulled me out of the habits, clutches, and roots that the enemy, and fear, had birthed in me, things I didn't realize were present.

I started going to church, and I soon started going to intercessory prayer. When I walked in, a lady named Romanza said, "God gave me a vision that you were going to be here." This statement began the journey of understanding prayer and developing a prayer language. As I developed in the spiritual realm, I was like a prayer crackhead. I prayed about everything. If I poured coffee in the morning, I said, "Oh, God, let this be the best cup I've ever had; let the cream and sugar be stirred in perfectly." I was a prayer addict. I was super faithful and the youngest person in the group. I was the youngest person who was a preacher. I was the youngest person who was dealing with the teens and youth, and I was barely older than them. I was on mute in the prayer ministry for years, so for my prayer group, I had to show up; I had to be consistent. I had to show up everywhere and be on time; if I wasn't, they would sit me down. But I never said anything; I was on mute. I had to be faithful in my training. People said, "You're great, you're always here, you're so faithful, look at you—you're so young, you're so this, you're so that." But they didn't know I was using church to escape; it was my new drug.

Great but Not Good Enough

The church's validation was giving me an identity. At each point in my life, whatever I escaped to was supposed to provide me with an identity. If you praise me for showing up on time, I am going to show up; I am going to show up super early, I am going to sleep at church. If you praise me for being with the teens and children, I am going to do it even more. I was doing all these things, and it looked like I was growing by leaps and bounds, that God was using me, but behind closed doors, I was a hot mess. But the gifts belong to him, and he can use them how he wants to. I was essentially using God. I had the form of God, which we often talked about in church, but it is what's beneath that sound of prayer, what's beneath that showing up. Nobody ever saw it.

After I got married and had my son, I had postpartum depression. Even before that, I did not want to have kids, and when I got married, I didn't want to have any more. So many things had happened, and I had a couple of abortions along the way.

When I got pregnant, I felt my husband had trapped me into staying married, and I spiraled then. I went to some of the mentor ladies in the church, and they told me I would get over it. But I didn't; I really didn't. Those first years with my son was a lot of work because my then-husband was in the military and was always gone. He lived in another state, and there was infidelity, which I didn't know about at the time. I went back to school, so it was a blur of work, and I was burned out. I was a shell of a person, but I looked like I was godly, I looked like I was a pillar and a rock, but inside, I was an imposter.

I had graduated with a BA, I had two master's degrees, and I was almost finished with the PhD program. Yet I never celebrated those successes because I always felt like what was going on behind closed doors was where I lived my life. Fear was always speaking to me, even though things came easily to me. I was good at multiple things, people liked me, and I was a loving person. I lived my life based on the decision that I was just a statistic, so I prayed so hard, showed up so hard, prophesied and gave so hard because I didn't know if when judgment day came, I would really go to heaven. I was twenty-seven years old, I was hardcore in church, hardcore for God, I was in church leadership, I had a preachers' collar around my neck, but when the rubber met the road, I wasn't sure if I would go to heaven.

I had the abortions, I'd done the drugs, I did people dirty along the way, and people got strung out on drugs because of me. Maybe if I just showed up and kept working, I would be okay. Maybe I could just work my way into grace. Maybe I could sacrifice everything to really show

God I was worthy of the stuff I prayed about and preached to others.

What Is Imposter Syndrome?

For many years, I felt as if I was an imposter. In my research, I found that there is an actual name for this—imposter syndrome. This is when you're doing well on the outside, but you feel like people are going to find out that you're a fraud on the inside.

Research has proven that imposter syndrome is real. Two American psychologists, Pauline Clance and Suzanne Imes, identified it in 1978. They described it as a feeling of "phoniness in people who believe that they are not intelligent, capable or creative despite evidence of high achievement." While these people "are highly motivated to achieve," they also "live in perpetual fear of being 'found out' or exposed as frauds."[1]

Maya Angelou shared the following in an interview: "I have written eleven books, but each time I think, 'Uh oh, they're going to find out now. I've run a game on everybody, and they're going to find me out.'"

We all get to the place of beginning a great work to bring to the world, and our thoughts begin to terrorize us. We ask questions, probing into our rights as creators, imposing upon our rights as human creators to be great. We enter into a situation where we must overcome ourselves—some part of us must die for another part of us to emerge. The emergence or genesis—bringing the invisible into the public and visible market, we battle again with vulnerability. Will the world accept my work? If they reject my work, inherently, they are rejecting me. Will they see me for the fraud I feel that I am?

"I've run a game on everybody, and they are going to find me out...."

We must arrest these thoughts and call them what they really are—fear. Fear of what is, what was, and what can be—fear. Fear of never making it, becoming the person we interact with in our head. Fear of making it so big we are rejected by the people who have loved us most faithfully. Fear of being judged. Fear of being changed. Fear of never being able to replicate success—being the dreaded one-hit wonder. Fear of competition. Fear of not competing. Fear we actually can have it all. We have wasted so much time living in fear that we are afraid to make the giant steps toward change because our identity would have to be reformed to fit into this new state of the soul—courage.

Notice this has nothing to do with skill, nothing to do with intelligence, nothing to do with capability, but it has everything to do with fear. Why must we remain mentally imprisoned, spiritually impoverished? Is this what we have earned? Smoke and mirrors, lies, deception, but a very real lived experience, shared experience, a rich experience because we all have a fear to get over and a story to work through.

The fear authenticates you. You are not an imposter. You are human. I am human. You are the real deal. You are a solution for humanity. You are wisdom. You are here.

I am not a life coach. No, I am a type and shadow of you—an extension of your purpose interconnected with your story.

Show me your certificate of authentication. What is your story?

"What lies behind you and what lies in front of you, pales in comparison to what lies inside of you."
—Ralph Waldo Emerson

However, the process that we touch, feel, and engage in is part of a bigger process. All of us have processes within a process that we don't talk about. We usually meet our intended audience after we have gained a level of success. People are drawn to the success, but they grow from the wisdom of your process.

The process is the pain, failures, admittance to personal vices and mental vices. The process levels the experience of humans being human.

There's another imposter. This whole "fake it till you make it" mindset is a lie. Shenanigans! I don't know where that came from, but I sure fell for it. Faking it was exactly what I did most times. The shame attached only pushed me further into the hands of fear because I was not being transparent and telling my story. I could have said, "This is who I was, and these are some of the things I did, but by the blood of Jesus and the grace of God, I'm standing in a new place." However, I continued being an imposter. I kept acting like things were okay. I kept acting like this church identity was the end all be all. I kept acting like I was this prayer guru. I was popping my collar, with my rapper chains. I was not an imposter for needing healing; I was an imposter for not being transparent about my need for healing. I was using God. I was using the Word, and I was using the gifts for my own glory. I was using these things to keep me hidden from really being seen.

I really didn't want to be alive. After being in the church, praying, preaching, and dealing with people's kids, I would go home behind closed doors and ask the Lord, "Why am I even here? What's the purpose of all this?" In those moments, God was saying, "I want to transform you, but I'm going to take you from this place and bring you to where I am."

It takes courage to cross over because the pain is comfortable. The misery is comfortable. The people are comfortable too because there is no accountability, no push for development; no one is adding a whole lot because they don't know me. I was able to maintain, even though I was horribly dissatisfied. Fear would speak and say, "Oh no, you're fine; you're good; you're okay. You can maintain by simply doing what you are doing to escape the truth,"... but you are dying.

Endnotes

---

[1] Oxford Reference, c.v. "imposter phenomenon," accessed June 12, 2019, https://www.oxfordrefer-ence.com/view/10.1093/oi/authority.20110803095959571.

What Exactly Is Courage?

— 4 —

When you are so broken you cannot be mended, when you are shattered beyond recognition, that is when you are ready to be made whole.

WE HAVE AN IDEA of what courage is when we're kids. We're given all these fairy tales, and the meat of the story of the hero's journey is that the hero is a regular person. The regular person is a coward in some area and needed their guide on the side, their Mr. Miyagi, to develop their courage. The development phases and processes we are introduced to through these narratives are also a fantasy. Through these fairy tales, we're handed courage repeatedly as kids, but courage in terms of how we view it versus how it's really defined are two very different things.

Courage in a Few Words

The word courage in Hebrew is *amet*, which means to confirm, be courageous, of good courage, steadfastly minded, strong, stronger, establish, fortify, harden,

It is a primitive root meaning to be alert, physically (on foot) or mentally (in courage)—confirm, be courageous (of good courage, steadfastly minded, strong, stronger), establish, fortify, harden, increase, prevail, strengthen (self), make strong (obstinate, speed).

> cour·age, /ˈkərij/Submit, noun
>
> The ability to do something that frightens one. "She called on all her courage to face the ordeal." Strength in the face of pain or grief.[2]

Another Hebrew word, *leb,* has the following meanings:[3]

Soul or heart of man

Conscience

Seat of appetite

Seat of emotions and passions

Seat of courage

Leb is the word for heart, and we look through all the faculties of the heart and mind, painting a picture of the inner workings of man. In the Old Testament, we find that the end of the list is the seat of courage. *Amet* is a noun and is the Hebrew word for courage. It means to be fortified, stronger, to establish, to be obstinate, to prevail, and to be steadfast in your mind. In terms of the fairy tale, we're taught that courage is the ability to do something that frightens you. This makes sense because you don't need courage unless you're scared, right? If you feel like you can accomplish it, you're not activating courage. But when we look at courage as being a seat of the soul, courage is a mindset.

Courage is an obstinate mindset that facilitates faith.

We can pray and we can talk about the gift of faith, which are things in the spirit realm—gifts of the spirit, but courage is the seat of the soul. Courage causes the unseen; whatever faith is to be applied to, and whatever action you have to engage in, all ride upon that seat of the soul, courage.

When we say faith without works is dead, courage is the foundation that faith and works are set upon. You can pray all day, and you could really have the faith. Many times people say, "God give me more faith," but it is not faith you need—it is really courage; it is the activating of the seat of the soul. Courage is dusting off that seat, dusting off that throne of the soul, and activating it so that your prayers of great faith and the activity that will be birthed because of those prayers now have a bridge, the unseen to the seen, the bridge is courage. My prayer life was smashed, and I was single for the first time in my adult life. I lost the home I owned. I lost two businesses because of where I was financially and mentally. Completion of my dissertation for my PhD was delayed.

I finally rose out of this funk, only to deal with the aftermath and the knowledge that life didn't stop. I woke up to a credit score of 512 and having to rent a townhouse double the mortgage of my old home. I hadn't worked for anybody other than myself in a long time, so my businesses dried up—all the way up. I used up everything and spent up everything. The aftermath was ridiculous.

I felt like a huge failure on top of everything else that was going on, but the depression was gone; God had rebuilt me. I see church totally different now. The world says put your money where your mouth is, but I had to put my mind where my mouth was because, in the church, we often say things that our minds don't believe. We say a lot of things that our minds are just not obstinate about. We say a lot of things where our minds are not fortified to the point of completion. The definition of courage is rooted in the idea that our minds are fixated on forward momentum even in the face of uncertainty and imminent failure. I had to live again. This is when I said, "Okay, God, let me feel all of this. Let me feel having terrible credit; let me feel what it's like to have almost two hundred thousand dollars in student loans that are now due. Let me feel what it's like to have to rename a business because the old business has been administratively dissolved. Let me feel all of this." I was in my thirties, and nobody expects to be dealing with stuff like this at that age—but then again, I could feel the pain, so there was hope for change.

Note to Self

Processing in this process…I have hit a wall.

A stone wall. I feel like this stone wall. I cry for this stone wall. Write about this stone wall? I don't know how at the present moment. I have lived in this stone casing for so long to now have to betray this relationship—as I deny and mourn this despicable death of an unspoken an ancient deception depicted as truth.

How do I begin to undo my internal DNA?

This inheritance is so deep that

I cannot even feel it vibrating in my bones.

So deep my own heart has bowed itself and does not recognize it as a stranger.

How do I begin to regrow in the soil of truth?

- Annice, Circa 2016.

Endnotes

[2] Lexico.com, *Oxford Dictionary* online, c.v. "courage," accessed June 12, 2019, https://www.lexico.com/en/definition/courage.
[3] The NAS Old Testament Hebrew Lexicon, c.v. "Leb," accessed June 12, 2019, https://www.biblestudytools.com/lexicons/hebrew/nas/leb.html.

The Grace of Pain

— 5 —

You can chase freedom, but fear causes you to run aimlessly behind it.

MANY TIMES IN OUR LIVES, courage is the fortification to keep walking. It is putting one foot in front of the other and continuing to move toward the destination or goal in front of you. I wasn't going to church anymore; I had been dropped by everyone, so I hooked up with this ministry and started giving prophetic words through email. I was still serving, but I didn't have to commute anymore.

When Periscope first came out, I heard the Lord saying, "You need to get on the pier and pray and teach." I looked a hot mess. I had acne, had lost hair, had low self-esteem, and experienced all kinds of crazy stuff. In the aftermath of everything being put back together, I remember saying, "Yeah, I know; I'm good on that." I would rather not go back into a place of judgment while I was still rebuilding me. How could I encourage people to keep going while I was still dealing with loss? Wouldn't I need to get my stuff together and then show up and speak to people from a place of wholeness? Can people be helped by someone who needed help?

Would my failures disqualify me from being a voice of wisdom to others? My paradigm was broken. While I had come through the worst of my process, my view on the process was broken still.

Courage.

The law of inertia states that an object in motion tends to stay in motion. The same rule applies to habitual courage or habitual cowardice. A linear pathway, while invisible to the natural eye, is distinct and blaring to the eyes of the subconscious. You must begin to retrain your mind so that it works for you and not against you in the times where you need courage.

Pain Producing Perception

Several months later, I got on Periscope and followed Apostle John Eckhart, and he shared content from Alexis Maston. I started watching her, and this young lady prophesied, did poetry, and told jokes. I admired her courage. People would say crazy stuff in the comments. Sophia Ruffin participated too. While I admired what they were saying, I was more mesmerized by their courage to get in front of people and live out loud. This began to spark a dormant place in me. There was this freedom I'd always been chasing while fear was causing me to run aimlessly behind it.

Bringing my work to the world was a *serious* challenge for me. I wrote little pieces and published them during off-peak hours—I knew no one would be reading at these times. Little by little, I gained more confidence that gave me the courage to write and publish more. However, my end goal was to publish videos and not just written work.

I desired true freedom to be and to live transparently. The freedom of "if you don't like it, don't look." The freedom of an "I do not care what others think or say" anointing.

Somehow, I started talking to Dr. Alexis, and one of the first things she said was I needed to be teaching on Periscope. I wanted to; I could taste it; it was freedom! It wasn't about actually doing live videos—it was the concept of exercising courage and being free. The idea scared me, and I had every excuse in the book as to why I could not. I had every reason why the timing was not right. It's never going to be right, it's not the right time, and I don't have the right equipment. I don't have the content. I do not have an audience. Ultimately, the only thing missing was my courage. The only way to be courageous is to actually be courageous.

The time came for me to begin making videos. I was struggling with posting pictures of myself online. I wrote articles…plenty of articles. The published articles did not seem to help me in terms of achieved success. Sometimes it helps to comb through experiences, sifting through all the frames to find hidden gems of truth. There I was, cowering behind the computer screen pumping out articles—really good articles that no one was reading. In my frustration, I stood in the mirror and began to talk to myself. That is where I had the aha moment.

There I stood, and in that moment, I was introduced to the courage of my soul. I'd always chucked up my decisions as being obstinate and stubborn. I never once considered this as being a bold and courageous move. To step out into the world baring it all, for all to judge. In that moment, staring into the mirror, something in me clicked. If I didn't care then, why, oh why, should I care now?

If I had the audacity then, why not have the audacity now? If I had the power to face what scared me then—why would I not have the power to face what was scaring me now? Is this not the definition of courage? Is this not the rhythm of courage? Is this not the sound of courage?

Every moment of our lives, we instinctually create action plans and programs for the future—anticipating the moment at hand, the next minutes, the emerging hours, the following days, the ongoing weeks, and the anticipated years to come—in one part of our minds.

These plans are sequentially organized, as a series of potential actions: "If this happens, I will do that." These are not predictions. They do not pretend to tell what will happen. They are time paths into an anticipated future.

"Not only does the brain make those time paths in the pre-frontal lobes, it stores them. We visit these futures and remember our visits. We have, in other words, 'a memory of the future, . . .' continually being formed and optimized in our imagination and revisited time and time again."

This process "apparently helps us sort through the plethora of images and sensations coming into the brain, by assigning relevance to them. We perceive something as meaningful if it fits meaningfully with a memory that we have made of an anticipated future. . . . The stored time paths serve as templates against which the incoming signals are measured. If the incoming information fits one of the alternative time paths, the input is understood. . . . We will not perceive a signal from the outside world unless it is relevant to an option for the future that we have already worked out in our imaginations. The more memories of the future we develop, the more open and receptive we will be to signals from the outside world."[4]

Working on memories for the future is worth taking a second to ponder. Oftentimes, we are not even aware of what we are thinking about—but what if we became aware that our brains are looking to create memories for future events? What if we purposefully participated in the process of creation? The more we visit certain memories, a level of weight is assigned to the future memory. The more weight assigned, the more the brain assigns importance to future memory. When we find ourselves in need of access to a memory, the associated emotions, and physiological state needed for the performance of the body, the brain will pick from the highest weighted future memories.

"We will not perceive a signal from the outside world unless it is relevant to an option for the future we have already worked out in our imaginations."[5]

We do not receive signals from the outside world unless it is relevant to the option for the future we have already worked out in our imaginations. The imagination is a powerful tool in our courage toolbox and confident weaponry. We use it already but mostly to work against us. We use our imaginations in times of worry. We create scenarios of the worst possible outcomes. When the stimulus is then presented to us in the outside world, we immediately gravitate toward it—only because we decided this was relevant and we have options already created for a time such as this.

What if we created options of power, creativity, joy, love, peace, and courage? What if we used our imaginations to create scenarios where we were amazing versions of ourselves? What if we refused to create scenarios with our imaginations representing our lower and base emotions? What if we were not looking for people to criticize our work? What if we were not expecting people to abandon us or reject us? What if...?

This is a wild notion, and I would be remiss if I did not mention the tactic I am introducing to you in some new-age, pie-in-the-sky, self-help mumbo jumbo. Marketers use these principles when creating scenarios for marketing decisions, creating scenarios for product placement in future circumstances across different marketing channels and audiences.

Employ these methodologies for getting your mind to work in sync with your brain and body.

We have an amazing creative ability inside of us. What you see right now in front of you in terms of purpose entering the world and being presented to the audience of humankind is only a tenth of what you are able to create and present.

Courage. Simplistic in terms of clarity. Complex in terms of practice. Really, we practice courage every day. We have the understanding to extract moments of courage to create a linear path for patterns of habit while creating future memories to trigger courage to immediately move into action at any given moment.

The cycle of success and confidence are tied together tightly. Research has shown the only way to build confidence is to keep building successes—success in terms of building knowledge and taking steps of action. Researchers call this the Confidence-Competence Loop.[6] The premise of the theory is quite simple yet profound in its truth.

It was never going to be right, and when an event arose, I had to do it. There was no way around it. I had to decide to just do it—no matter the outcome. The first couple of videos weren't my best work, but even still, I tasted freedom and courage. It was like something in my soul clicked, and I became obstinate about being free no matter what.

Pain Producing Purpose

In any relationship, even with my kids, if they start saying something and I feel like ropes are being tied around my legs, feet, or hands, I will immediately break it. Even when entering into a business contract or covenant, there should be the freedom to be who we are and have this freedom show up in our juice. We're still morphing, we're still becoming, and we're marching forward, but there's just this freedom, this liberty. The Bible talks about the blessing of Abraham over Naphtali as a confirmation that he was a hind let loose (Genesis 49.21). He was free.

After going through the divorce, I had stopped preaching, I stopped praying, and I even stopped doing the prophecies by email. People would invite me, but I declined. I was bitter and didn't need to touch anybody, pray for anybody, or talk to anybody. I didn't want to be around people. When I started doing the videos, I had freedom—that's what God was giving me. He smashed my life, including my prayer life, because it was not of him. Most of it was churchy shenanigans, and most of the stuff I was teaching was binding people. It was not loosing them to the freedom of Jesus Christ. I had to go through this elaborate, crazy season because I didn't want to go willingly. If anybody could tell me what I was saying was wrong, the modality, the vehicle, I was using was error. It was wrong because it was binding, it was not God. Just because you can find it in Scripture does not mean you have the spirit of God.

I was doing these terrible live videos, but I felt so free! And I feel one of the ministries God has given me is freedom, liberty! Even if you are skeptical about your freedom, I believe there's such a spirit of liberty and freedom in flying and flowing in your God-given rights of being a child and heir in the inheritance of Jesus Christ. We've been some places, we've done some things, we've hurt some people; but at the end of the day, we're not the sum total of what we've done. We are the sum total of what he's done, and there is such liberty and freedom to be and to become and to keep being and to keep becoming.

Confidence

"Confidence is full trust; belief in the powers, trustworthiness, or reliability of a person or thing: We have every confidence in their ability to succeed. 2. belief in oneself and one's powers or abilities; self-confidence; self-reliance; assurance."[7]

Belief in your ability to succeed is the main weapon against fear. Belief in your ability spurs you to action. Action places distance between you and fear. Fear creates a perfect environment for excuses. Excuses open the door for procrastination. Procrastination steals, kills, and destroys potential. Diminished potential lowers the probability of living your purpose. Not truly living your purpose is not truly living.

The research attributes competence as an easily achieved confidence hack. The more you learn, the more you practice, the more you will gain momentum. Momentum is activity. Momentum is confidence in action. Fear cannot penetrate momentum.

You need momentum. The more you feel like you are getting better at whatever you are doing, you are experiencing levels of success. The great thing about success is size does not matter! The brain treats all success like success and begins to send signals to ease you into having more instances of success. The brain has a big ego. Tap into it and create success and the brain will begin to support your efforts.

What does this look like? It is learning subject matter in your area of expertise. Find ways to test yourself in small increments. The more you learn, the more your confidence begins to build. Every time you retain and regurgitate or implement your newly acquired knowledge, your brain responds favorably.

A Recovering Coward

Now, four years later, I need to convey the message that I have not made it; I'm still on the road. I say to people jokingly, "Hi, my name is Annice, and I used to be a coward." I'm absolutely a recovering coward in terms of revealing and being authentically who I am and how God made me. Right now, I'm still becoming, and I'm still on the road. I have not reached the ultimate courage fountain, but I have peace. I'm still unfolding, but if I had to go back from the beginning and do it all over again, I absolutely would. I would be a little girl praying for God to send me my real parents; I would watch my dad die again; I would go through the spiral and the abortions. That was bad decision-making, but the aftermath of the bad relationships and the abusive marriage helped me understand that this was my grace. This is grace.

I believe that the favor of God is seen in this story. A lot of the stuff that we call a blessing is not even a blessing; a lot of the stuff that we call a blessing is really a Band-Aid. It's what you're supposed to be moving; it's what you're supposed to be producing and is not a blessing. It is a command that is over your life. When I look at Joseph and see him in the pit, I see favor. When I look at him in Potiphar's house, I don't see only a slave; I see the favor of God resting on him to go through such shenanigans and still come out and get to walk in his God-ordained mandate. All these things, all these faces, all the brokenness, the broken heart, the broken life, and the broken finances, to me that's favor. It was favor that the Holy Spirit was struggling with me so that he kept me and I did not curse God and die. That's favor! When I was supposed to die in certain situations, there was God, like Job's three friends, sitting with me while I went through those situations and he kept me. That's favor!

At this place, I wish I could run back through the pages of my life and meet with and call the people who broke my heart, did not give me what I felt they were supposed to give me, and used me. I wish I could shake their hands and say thank you. They were the key to unlock the door to this place of courage and freedom. I always say that Joseph's brothers were the key to open the door of his destiny.

A few months after my divorce, my hair started falling out and my skin broke out. Every inch of my face was scarred, discolored, and covered in painful acne. I never dealt with anything like this before and was clueless to what was going on...completely clueless. How could a grown woman develop acne? For the space of four years I prayed, spent money, and mixed ingredients in hopes of finding a solution for my skin and hair. Those experiences would become a company of products and services women have described as a personal answer to prayer for their own skin and hair. Pretty Naked Skincare is the byproduct, the love child, or a key of grace masked in the fortune of heartbreak.

My mom and I still rarely talk. She still cusses me out and tells me bad things about myself, but I no longer expect her to treat me a certain way. Now I pray, "God, this is your daughter, and she's never tasted these sides of you. Let her taste these sides of you before she leaves the earth." I'm grateful to have come through her womb and to have felt her pain and the brunt of her pain because I got to meet the sides of God that would not have been available if I did not go down this particular path. You would not get to meet with the sides of God that can never be taken from you. There are some places in your life where you know it was only God. The favor of these situations allows us to meet with the sides of him to know him in his dimensions and depth.

I'm grateful for people and places, so I admonish you to reframe your memories; that's how memories get healed. Pray that God will heal memories and reframe them. Often, we are looking at something through our own experiences and through our own expectations that we built; they're not expectations built by the expectation of God, and when the expectation of God meets your expectations, it overcomes your expectations, and your eyes are open. You can look at your past situation and what was a memory that used to speak and yell and cuss and fuss at you is now a memory that you can look at and say, "My gosh! I wouldn't change it for a thing because this was the gateway; this was the portal; this was the door to God-grace."

Endnotes

[4] Arie de Geus, *The Living Company: Habits for Survival in a Turbulent Business Environment* (Boston: Harvard Business School Press, 2002), 35–36.
[5] Ibid.
[6] See "The Confidence/Competence Loop," *Leadership & Learning with Kevin Eikenberry* (blog), accessed June 12, 2019, https://blog.kevineikenberry.com/leadership-supervisory-skills/the-confidencecompetence-loop.
[7] Dictionary.com, c.v. "confidence," accessed June 12, 2019, https://www.dictionary.com/browse/confidence.

Courage Activation

— 6 —

The best way to be courageous is to be courageous.

Deuteronomy 31:6 NKJV

Be strong and of good courage, do not fear nor be afraid of them; for the Lord your God, He is the One who goes with you. He will not leave you nor forsake you.

Joshua 1:3–9

I promise you what I promised Moses: "Wherever you set foot, you will be on land I have given you. … No one will be able to stand against you as long as you live. For I will be with you as I was with Moses. I will not fail you or abandon you. Be strong and courageous, for you are the one who will lead these people to possess all the land I swore to their ancestors I would give them. Be strong and very courageous. … Study this Book of Instruction continually. Meditate on it day and night so you will be sure to obey everything written in it. Only then will you prosper and succeed in all you do. This is my command—be strong and courageous! Do not be afraid or discouraged. For the Lord your God is with you wherever you go.

1 Chronicles 28:20

David also said to Solomon his son, "Be strong and courageous, and do the work. Do not be afraid or discouraged, for the Lord God, my God, is with you. He will not fail you or forsake you until all the work for the service of the temple of the Lord is finished."

Psalm 27:1

The Lord is my light and my salvation; whom shall I fear?

The Lord is the strength of my life; of whom shall I be afraid?

Isaiah 41:10 NIV

So do not fear, for I am with you; do not be dismayed, for I am your God. I will strengthen you and help you; I will uphold you with my righteous right hand.

Isaiah 41:13

For I am the Lord, your God, who takes hold of your right hand and says to you, do not fear; I will help you.

Romans 8:15

For ye have not received the spirit of bondage again to fear; but ye have received the Spirit of adoption, whereby we cry, Abba, Father.

2 Timothy 1:7

For God has not given us a spirit of fear and timidity, but of power, love, and self-discipline.

1 John 4:18

There is no fear in love. But perfect love drives out fear, because fear has to do with punishment. The one who fears is not made perfect in love.

Psalms 27:14

Wait for the Lord; be strong and let your heart take courage; yes, wait for the Lord.

Matthew 14:27

Immediately Jesus spoke to them, saying, "Take courage, it is I; do not be afraid."

Psalms 18:39

You have girded me with strength for battle; you have subdued under me those who rose up against me.

Isaiah 41:6

Each one helps his neighbor and says to his brother, "Be strong!"

Strength and *courage* are synonymous in the Hebrew language. This is a list of the Scriptures that declare this. If you can find a strengthened prophetic narrative, you can find a courage truth. When you hold a courage truth, you are holding an activation in your hand. Activation is synonymous with victory.

A victory-consistent lifestyle is a courage-rich lifestyle.

To show up is courage. To stand is victory.

In order to stand you have to show up.

Satan is after your showing-up. When you do not show up, victory cannot stand…victory is forfeited. You were not overcome; you forfeited the victory. There's a big difference.

The Bible is clear: Decree (*decide* in Hebrew) a thing and it (the thing) will be established.

Activation is a decision. The declaration is the *how,* or directional piece of instructions associated with the decision.

Decision (Decree)

Before we open our mouths, let us straighten our minds.

What do you believe about the victory available to you?

What do you honestly and radically believe about what the Scriptures have declared?

Go back and reread the Scriptures. Can you make a decision about the declaration or decision and will of God concerning you?

In the space below, write your Confession of Decision.

CONFESSION OF DECISION

On this day of________ in the year of _______, I, _______________, make a declaration of decision concerning the Word of God and the courage markings of my soul.

I Believe

I Believe

I Believe

I Believe

I Believe

Signature

____

Date

____

Prayers

A Prayer of Repentance

Father, in the name of Jesus, I repent where I have quenched the Holy Spirit by turning a deaf ear to the plea to arise and shine. I repent where I have chosen the pride of satisfying self over being obedient at all costs. I repent in the name of Jesus for the sound of sin and the scent of sin surrounding my assignment on the earth. I repent for when I cried out to be used by you and then refused to go. Father, please forgive me. The name of Jesus is my safe and strong tower; I plead the name of Christ and the blood of Christ. I ask you to remove this burden of iniquity from my bloodline and my lineage and allow this case against me to be passed to the courts of mercy.

Thank you, merciful and kind judge, for banging the gavel on my behalf in favor of your Word and your good pleasure concerning my life.

I receive the full pardon.

In Jesus's name only…amen

A Prayer for the Outbreak of New Nature

Father, in the name of Jesus, blood of Jesus, words of Jesus, I agree in harmony to function in outbreak in this place of living on the other side of breakthrough. I accost this sound, source, and security that is embedded in the marching-forth orders within the royal decree concerning this time of my life. I arise within the anointing, authority, and authorship of your providential will. I sign my name as being the owner and administrator of eruption, upsurge, outburst, explosion, burst, and flurry. I understand these are the defining activities for this season associated with my name and the calling of my name by you. I agree and partner with the calling of my name. I agree and partner with your decision for using me in these ways. I acknowledge the *outbreak* anointing and breaker anointing associated with the calling.

I suit-up in you.

In *you* I live, move, and have my very being…*outbreak.*

In Christ…*for* Christ…*by* Christ…and *only* Christ…

Selah and Amen.

A Prayer for Redeeming Time

Father, in Christ's name, I receive this revelation of courage and outbreak past my intellectual capacity as human. You are a Spirit, so I agree with and encounter your *dabar* (Word) as spirit and life-giving favor. I take the constraints of my life and times and let them rest in your hands. My identity bows and worships as you crown me with understanding and purpose. I am not bound by a twelve-month cycle—I am constrained *only* in the freedom of the eternal breath of your Word over me. I am free…and I set your *dabar* free in me as a kingdom compass to point and appoint paths of righteousness for *your namesake.*

I am free because you created freedom and allow me to be set in freedom by Christ.

Selah.

A Prayer for Joy in Building Your New Courageous Life

Father in the name of Jesus, I readily receive my *joy* again. I do not want to tire in the middle of the process. I am grateful to be a builder in this season of the history of heaven. I am grateful to have a place, a calling, and a mandate to labor for the wall of heaven in the earth. God, I acknowledge your Holy Spirit work in me called *joy*.

I interact with *joy* right now in praise.

I declare the sound of *joy* will be my song. My song will be a strong song—a sound of deliverance in harmony with *your* song over my life. *Our* songs will have the same words and sounds, and they will make a great sound in the earth. God, you can trust me with *joy*. I will be an administrator of *joy* for the other builders. I will walk in the strength of this *joy* this season. I will fight for *joy*, and I will fight with *joy*.

I will build the wall.

I will not be feeble.

I will be a strong builder.

In Jesus's name.

Decrees

Decree of Activation

In the name of Christ, the person of Christ, and the character of Christ, this day on earth, courage is emerging in me. I am putting on the mandate to take heart. I am putting on the command to be strong only. I am girding my life with the relentless sword of God, which sets me in a place of strength only.

I put on the hidden and secret place of God, and I speak with boldness the secret counsels of God. My hands are instruments of prayer and war. My feet are purposed for victory and winning.

Timidity is not found in the person of Christ. Tenacity is found in the person of Christ.

Fear is not found in the person of Christ, but faith is found in the person of Christ.

Hiding is not found in the person of Christ, but higher is found in the person of Christ.

I am putting on the nature of Christ and the character of Christ like a garment. I am permitting the mind, thoughts, and patterns of Christ to also be in me and be found coming out of me. I am not erratic nor cowering; I am arising and shining in the *light* of God's dear Son.

I take the scroll of my life and open it in the earth. The sound of my lineage doing the bidding of God is released into the earth. The sounds of the *dabar* (words, work, books, instruction, writings, publishing, proclamations, business, and all business matters) of God are written upon the scroll being released. I set my mouth to be a river, I set my tongue to be a pen, I set my hands to be tools, and I set my life as an offering. I understand this complete yes is attached to the sound of keys being given to me to unlock doors in the kingdom of heaven. I understand that now as I decide as a governmental structure set in the earth, my words carry the weight of a judicial system, which cannot be challenged. I understand as a key-holding deputy that it is my charge to move *only* in courage and *take* the *land* which has been given to my fathers as an inheritance.

Decrees to My Memories

My past includes every measure of mistake, mistaken identity, and mishap by my hand and the hands of others and has produced "good" as spoken in Genesis. Good has satisfied God. Alongside this truth, every problematic start and every problematic season was the hand of God and the arm of God flexing in the earthly realm. God decided to use me. God decided to use me…and then heal me. God decided to use me, heal me, and then seal my healing. I am the recipient and the participant of the true favor of God and true grace of God. I was not born broken; rather, I was born with a blessing that would be a sword against deception in the earth. My life is a testimony, my times and seasons are a testimony, and my perceived brokenness is a testimony…he is God.

The I Am of Jehovah speaks over and about my life. Memories, I declare you are healed, as now I see and understand. The knowledge of truth I receive over my days.

Today is the day. I have arisen. My lineage also with me has arisen. We bulldoze ahead in the courageous nature of almighty Jehovah.

Selah. In Christ's name.

Decree of Comprehension

Father in the name of Jesus, the name by which I live, move, and have my existence, I am deciding to—on purpose, with forethought and afterthought—put on the composure of Christ, the comprehension of Christ, the understanding of Christ through faith…today.

I comprehend that as I put on this mind, I am literally putting on you.

I comprehend that I as I authorize this comprehension, I am putting on every decree of the Scripture.

I understand I am standing in, standing under, and standing with the affirmations of victory that you are.

I am permitting the Word to speak over my day.

I am allowing the power of heaven to overtake my hands.

I am sanctioning the creativity of the Creator to have reign in the domain of my life (Matthew 6:33).

I am empowering every dormant jot and tittle of the breath of God to blow upon my person.

I grant the rights of the inheritance to the victory that is the name of Jesus to be my portion. Hourly, this is my portion.

I submit the decrees of my mouth to the decree of God's mouth. We decree in harmony. We decree in unity.

There is one sound over my days, and the days of my lineage—the sound of victory.

– Selah, amen.... It is finished...in his name.

I Ain't There, but I Ain't There Either

— 7 —

Courage is the resistance to fear, the mastery of fear not the absence of fear. – Mark Twain

WE TALKED ABOUT HAVING this obstinate mindset in putting your mind where your mouth is so you can stop being unstable. It's a mindset. Stability is birthed out of a mindset, so where there is instability, there is courage, the seat soul, if you will, that says I am stoppable. I am this, and I am that, I am not, and I don't measure up.

You're judging yourself instead of judging the God in you. I think for this to stick and stay, that's what it's all about: one thing, one message. You are courageous. You will not always be successful, and not everything you put your hands to will have the outcome you want. It will prosper according to the expectation of God, but that may not be the outcome you want. Sometimes God is producing character in us, and this is the purpose of an assignment. The assignment-outcome failed according to our standards, but it was a home run according to God's standards because what was produced in you will bring forth the glory.

I am ready for this freedom, this courage, this mindset to stick and stay. There has to be a consistent soul reflection where we hold the seats of our souls, the thrones of our souls, because that's exactly what they are, thrones. We hold the seats of our soul up against the character of God and against the Word of God. Even if you only have one word right and don't have a whole lot of the Word, you have a whole lot of the presence of God. Live your life according to the measure of the Word of the Lord that you know. The presence of God is a full measure of himself that you allow in. Even if you feel like you have a whole lot of the Word, make sure you have a whole lot of his presence. Take these seats, these thrones of your soul, and measure them not against you but against who he is. The presence is so big it occupies every throne of your soul.

Now the question is not do I measure up? It is what is seated on these thrones and what is his character? The Bible says if we resist the devil, he will flee from us (James 4:7). Fear was driving me, but now it has been cast out. However, fear is still a hunter. It still speaks, it still screams, and it still barks. Sometimes I still have those moments where I want to falter, where I want to fall back. Being an addict is going back to something; going back to being a coward is really seductive—going back to a quiet place, going back to where nobody sees you, where you can just hide in the shadows. But this is where the bondage of fear will come against you, so anytime fear rolls up on the property, I do a soul reflection, and then I must move into the framework of what I know. I've got to stay free at all costs, so the things I don't do are the things that fear says not to do because I will fail. I take that seat of the soul called courage and lift it before the Father because I know it isn't about the outcome—it's about my worship.

If only two people read this book and one of them is you and the other one is your mama, it's okay because it's not about the outcome of success with people; it is about the outcome of obedience. Every time I'm obedient, the seat of the soul is widened a little bit more, expanded a little bit more. I am, and you must also be, on this epic obedient adventure that wherever the sound of God, the presence of God, and the voice of God takes us, whatever his requirements of us, we're not looking at what people will say in terms of success or failure, but we're looking to do it so we can be in this place. My life with my hands lifted in worship, saying I surrender, saying *God I may not be able to trace you, but I trust you*—that's what obedience is.

Sole Reflection

When we talk about the soul reflection—S.O.U.L.— there's also the S.O.L.E. reflection, when your life is lived for an audience of one. We must fight to stay in that place. I'm a wife for an audience of one; I'm a husband for an audience of one. Everybody gets the benefit—the world may get the benefit, your husband may get the benefit, but at the end of the day, I'm doing this before the audience of one. There is such a freedom and the courage to repent, to relent, to forget, to open a business, and write a book. The audience of one now becomes my worship, my courage, and my soul makes it boast; every seat of my soul is boasting in the Lord. Whatever he says has a bridge, and so when we pray, "Thy kingdom come; thy will be done," it will definitely happen because the bridge is open, so this is going to stick and stay. This is the concept if you're dealing with fear. When I pray, I see myself flying and see myself doing great things, and when I come back to myself, I am horrified. The only way to get past it, the only way to do it, is to do it; the only way to have courage is to have courage.

Your Courage

The one thing that could really transform you and help you move from fear to courage is just one step. The moment you write out an outline for a live video, the moment you sit down and start drawing up the plans and make the phone call for the business, this is the moment when you cross over. It's not a big thing; it's really just a series of small things, but those small things make your whole life a life of worship. The audience of One—God—is overtaking everything. With God sitting on the throne of your life, you will begin to see yourself consistently punching fear in the face as you light a courage-fire in the people you come in contact with.

My clients have often referred to me as their life coach. Funny, I am your business coach who believes in building radical fishermen so your legacy can eat indefinitely. Sure, my methodology for working with my clients does take on the look of life coaching. It is a rather intimate approach; they allow me to see their hidden places they allow no one else accesses. However, I do not consider myself a life coach.

Mentor—maybe.

I understand where this belief comes from. I can see how the mix-up happens. In order for me to design a platform for your product, I must first excavate the phantom problematic paradigms of pitiful principles prophesied inwardly, silently, and secretly by your secret self.

I excavate the soul. I become your soul archeologist. The most valuable market your product will grace is the place of your person...your purpose. The truth is the product will only go as far as the perceived efficacy.

"Can I do this?"

"Do I have what it takes?"

Everyone has hidden gems of ideas within them. Daily, you think of at least ten amazing things that could change the world...but like birds, these ideas take flight and fly away. Why? Because of how you view your own ability to actually produce what you see inside of yourself. These ideas originated from inside of you; therefore, everything needed to bring the vapor of idea into concrete manifestation also resided in the place of origination, inside of you.

What if for every idea that comes across the desk of your mind, you already knew you had the answers, solutions, and energy to make it happen? What if the only question to be answered was whether or not the time to accomplish this particular idea was now?

What if you knew your purposeful identity? Every person has a purpose, but every purpose has a person.

It looks like the same idea but understanding the distinction separates the fulfilled from the unfulfilled. It is the line of demarcation, separating the ordinary from extraordinary, the good from the great, the human from the divine; all rests within the bosom of this one truth.

We must begin a dig. We must find the artifacts and fossils of your species. These are not the usual questions we love to answer or dig for: Who are we and why are we here?

My question: What are you?

Defined in the what is the who and the why. What are you?

Look at your trip to earth within the boundless limits of your purpose calling for you to fulfill it—not it fulfilling you. Your purpose calls for you to bring life to it—not for it to bring life to you. Your purpose births you—not the other way around. Your purpose was here first.

The garden existed and then Adam was created—for the garden.

So we dig. What are you? We must begin at the beginning. What are the motivations—the drivers behind your current life situations? We burrow through dirt and rocks, understanding this process only works if we get dirty. We all have some dirt and mud on us. We all have some residue from things present in our lives, which we really do not want.

What we do not want is a key to understanding our identity. What we do not want is a key to understanding what we are built to take down and built to take over. Starting in the miry places is the only way to hit the gold hidden underneath. Often, because we are seeking to answer why we are here, we limit ourselves to the answers we see around us in our experience.

If a sink was seeking to understand why it existed. The sink may limit the answer to washing things and providing water. This is only a fraction of the answer. This sink is part of a bigger network—a kitchen or bathroom—and is vital to the overall purpose of the environment it is placed in. The sink only scratched the surface by answering in terms of functionality and not identity.

Your identity is not limited to function.

There is a depth we have yet to unlock when we describe our professions as lives. You are not a stay-at-home mom; you are selfless servant consumed with the welfare of your community (small and broad) in the present and for the future. You will not rest; you will die pouring yourselves into human beings called out of your loins of legacy.

Summing up the totality of existence in terms of perceived functionality becomes a static limitation. Your human abilities are always expanding, and there are no limits to the levels of expansion. The only limit comes when you do not do the necessary digging to find out what you truly are and the ecosystems you are vitally a part of.

Much of what we think and how we operate is smoke and mirrors. Behind all this stuff you presented to the world, if it is not in line with the call of your purpose, then you are struggling, wrestling, grappling, fighting what seems to be shadows in the darkness. You do not understand the resistance—yet the resistance is there and very real.

What is your fight? What thoughts are you battling against, constantly?

Let me help you.

You stare at your purpose, face to face. You see the end—wild and wonderful filled with vision as you move about in passionate pursuit of promising profitable prosperity (nothing missing, nothing lacking, and nothing broken) centered around a particular people. This task will change the world of those whom this purpose will touch. You have touched life. Your heart beats in harmony with an ancient legacy far beyond your finite moment.

You hesitate. You tell yourself you are not enough, not worthy combined with not skilled, crafty, intelligent, or courageous enough. The truth is you feel ashamed. In the shadows of all the not enough-ness is a deeper moment—shame. You look out into a world of people who are amazing, wonderful, and intelligent. What is the difference between them and you? Perhaps they did things the right way. Perhaps they work hard, burning the candle at both ends.

You ask yourself: "Do I have what it takes to sustain?" "Am I just a dreamer?" "Will people even accept me and my work as valid and necessary?" These are all valid questions. Honestly, we all must sit down and count the costs associated with such a great purpose. However, consider the motive for asking the questions, the tone of these questions. Are these even questions we are really looking for an answer to or rather statements of emphatic self-proclaimed prophecy we are expecting that has already fulfilled itself?

My Truth

I was a parent before I graduated high school. I was homeless in my first college attempt, so I dropped out. I counted myself as a statistic. I judged my future with a standard of shame. I was just another girl who would live a life of strain and struggle, all bought on by my own hands. I was the perpetrator as well as the victim. I settled there for years—accepting a bitter life as my portion.

Then I fell back into college. I was grateful for a seat in my college courses. I was grateful for the opportunity of education. Yet I still moved forward with the stench of shame. Even at the doctoral level, having accomplished numerous scholastic awards, I was ashamed. So I never walked across a collegiate stage; I never displayed any of my multiple degrees and awards. I hid them in boxes. I hardly spoke of my accomplishments because I labeled myself an imposter. I told myself that my greatness would always be marred by inadequate behavior. My purpose was left naked and uncovered. I was left fruitless and barren. I was an imposter. Surely my purpose could just move on and choose someone who made no mistakes—a human who was perfection.

Here is the thing most great people may never tell you. At some point, we all have felt like an imposter. We have all stood on stages where we did not feel we had earned the right to grace. We have all sat across from someone we admired or someone we wanted to admire us and waited for someone to point a finger of accusation at us revealing the blaring truth.

Note to Self

Hey girl,

Here is what I found, and this is another side of the coin to consider as I determine the final judgment for what I have actually done with my life in my present state.

I am forty. Married twice. Divorced twice. Depressed multiple times. I own a business or two, and I have closed a business or three. I preach God, and I pray for people. I lost my fervency a few times, but I gained perseverance. I had my first child at seventeen. I have been homeless. I have owned homes. I have lost everything.

I have lived.

I have freaking lived. Yes, my life did not go as planned. I wonder whether I even had a plan as I came from a tumultuous beginning. However, I have beheld life. I have felt the events of brokenness and wholeness, death and birthing.

I have lived.

I have amassed what the world would call success. I have amassed grief, which produced a gratefulness that cannot be understood unless you have stood under the bridge of brokenness. I have been broken.

I have lived.

You have lived. Your stories of turmoil are stories of triumph. We see we are made of all things precious and gold. We can withstand the fire and come out perfect, weighty, and priceless. Yes, we pay a price for this type of glory. The glory to walk through the pain. The glory to walk through rejection. The glory to walk through life and wander through the "Valley of Decision" and judge what we have done with what we have been given.

The elegance of your experience is what energizes the world. The juice of life is in the journey of life. Success is measured in increments of inspiration. Baby girl, I am inspired by your journey and your experience gives wind to my wings.

Where I am is where I need to be—where I am graced to be.

You have touched many lives along the way. You are a minister of hope, and your life preaches realness.

Annice, you are doing good.

Love,

Yourself

The Taming of the Lion—You

The lion tamer is courageous, calm, and even crazy. We have all watched the lion roar while the lion tamer stands calmly—flicking the whip as we stare in awe, wondering.

How can a lion be controlled by something smaller and weaker? How can this king, this beast be controlled, which when met in the wild, could snap this weaker vessel in half in a matter of seconds? How has the tamer managed to strip the power from the lion?

How is this possible? Life. We find ourselves gazing back at the loss of time, the frailty of potential, depleting youthfulness, and we wonder how the lion in us became so powerless. There was a day where we knew we were invincible, a time where we were the king of our domains—even if just in our heads. We were unstoppable. We were a beast. How is this possible? As we study the methodology of the tamer, we find the process responsible for our weakening and the pricelessness of our remedy—the cage, and the stool.

You are the lion. Your purpose is the lion. Your potential is the beast. Your courage is the ferociousness. The cage is your paradigm shifting. The tamer represents disappointments, worldviews, foundational family origins, failed relationships, and any foreign entities impeding your true innate nature of ruler-ship. Authentically, you were created to rule your specific domain.

The Cage

There is a specific process for disarming a beast. The lion is roughly four times the size of the tamer, ferocious by nature, and intuitive to certain sights, sounds, and smells. The tamer employs disarming instincts and domesticates the lion's innate ferociousness through a battery of actions designed to remove this king from his throne.

The cage is used to introduce the lion to the tamer—introducing a finger, a hand, and a leg until the tamer can fully enter the cage and the lion will not attack because the lion has been systematically conditioned to the presence of this foreign body. The longer the process of introduction and induction, the longer this free species is in a confinement, which is slowly introducing domestication and familiarity with an unnatural relationship.

What feels, smells, and looks unnatural in your sphere? Where do you find yourself playing pretend? Pretending to be docile, pretending to be lesser, smaller, or weaker? Where have you fallen victim and cannot seem to recover from the victim mindset? What have you become familiar with that not only has you in a cage but is the ruler of that cage? You were created free—freedom is the innate and default setting in your mind, body, and spirit. What has invaded your purpose and potential domain? What or who is an unnatural connection?

Where are you not free?

The Stool

The tamer, once inside the cage with the beast, uses a stool or a chair to paralyze the beast. The lion cannot focus on one leg of the stool but attempts to focus on all four stool legs simultaneously. The lion becomes confused with these foreign objects—the trainer and his four-legged stool—in his environment. During this time of confusion, the tamer can introduce all sorts of commands for submission, which, in this case, represent the purposeful slaughter of courage. The lion is eventually under the control of what he could easily annihilate in seconds with little effort.

Confusion is sneaky. Wherever sincere clarity is not resting, confusion is spreading. Oftentimes, we make wishes and call them goals. Mistaking these as goals, we assume clarity is built in automatically. The reality is we are not clear on the objectives of the goals, the pathways of the goals, the resources of the goals.... We are confused.

The confusion then begins to leak into every area where clarity has not been achieved—without you even knowing. Soon you are moving in all directions, which are leading nowhere fast. You are stuck. You are sinking. Your purpose is experiencing slaughter, and your potential is exhausted from all the bustle of nonsense. The lion is being conquered. You are losing your roar. You are being conditioned to purr—unnaturally.

- Are you a lion who has forgotten the place from which it was taken, attempting to adapt and arrive in a realm it is either meant to control and rule or a place it should never be?
- Is this you? Conditioned, controlled, and consumed by the lesser?
- Has your roar has been snuffed out?
- Where have you set goals without clear direction?
- What journeys are you currently traveling that were never created to be included in this trip called your life?

King of the Jungle

It is time. It is time to wake up. The call of freedom is beckoning you back to rule your domain as it was intended. You are mighty as a lion.

The Peace of Courage

What you do with your creativity will shake the world. What you do with your potential will free a generation of captured lions. What you do to this lion tamer will place you back on your throne.

Welcome back.

– Annice, Circa 2018.

Your Courageous New Beginning

— 8 —

Now it's your turn.

IT'S YOUR TURN to write your own story. Not a story that is without bumps and bruises. Not a story that is without ups and downs, mountain-tops and valley lows. Rather, it is a story that is riddled with courage. A story of tenacity, faith, and the courage to conquer what scares you.

My story is your story, and your story is my story. What you have encountered throughout our time together was a simple journey of every human becoming their own sort of super-empowered hero in their everyday life. These pages were our living memoirs—the story of the human plight of acknowledging what scares us and our decision to fight against fear.

Now is when you make the decision; now is when you take what you've been activated in and apply it to your life. Now is the time where you take the activation and turn it into action in this physical world and do great exploits for the King.

Every day you are going to have to choose courage.

Every single day you are going to have to choose to wake up and activate the courage on the inside of your soul. The seat of courage must be aroused daily.

Every day you're going to have to fight through feelings of inadequacy, feelings of imposter syndrome, feelings of not being enough, feelings of not having the proper credentials. You're going to have to fight through the feelings.

Here it is. Your turn. This blank space is your canvas. Write a vivid story of what walking in your courage looks like, sounds like, and feels like.

Who is with you?

Who has moved on from you?

What habits have you had to develop?

What habits have you had to walk away from? Use this blank space as the prophetic second chance to be epic.

EMAIL YOUR STORY TO ME.

I would love to include your courage decision on my blog. I would love to be your courage partner. Let us walk together in this journey of courage. Email: annice@annicesilimon.com.

About the Author

Annice is a doctorate candidate in marketing, operates Growing Bright Ideas as a strategy consultant for small business and ministries, and is the creator of Pretty Naked Skincare Products. Annice is intentionally breaking barriers in multiple industries and paving the way so Christian businesses can have longevity in every aspect of their God space.

As a prayer strategist, Annice desires to see the prayer lives of people ignited with a fire which cannot be extinguished. Biblical truths implemented with practical methods prove to make for an experience of power and purpose exploding with possibility. Through various modalities, both spiritual and secular, the message of communing with God through relationship is the power of her mission. Annice's first book on prayer, *Irrevocable: Prayers and Decrees of Psalm 91*, was released in 2017.

Annice is the mother of two children who have been tasked by God to raise their mother, and they are doing a fantastic job.

Follow Annice

Facebook: Annice Silimon

Website: annicesilimon.com

Email: annice@annicesilimon.com

Can You Help?

Reviews are everything to an author because they mean a book is given more visibility. If you enjoyed this book, please review it on your favorite book review sites and tell your friends about it. Thank you!